Birds
of
Berkeley

Birds
of
Berkeley

Written and illustrated by

Oliver James

Heyday, Berkeley, California

Thanks to the following photographers, whose photographs
informed the illustrations:

American Robin © Dave Spates
Anna's Hummingbird © Tom Sanders
Bufflehead © Chris Lue Shing
Black Phoebe © Bill Holsten
European Starling © Jason Jablonski
Forster's Tern © Trent Bell
Golden-crowned Sparrow © Tom Grey
Oak Titmouse © Greg Lavaty
Red-breasted Nuthatch © Earl Orf
Ruby-crowned Kinglet © Maria De Bruyn
Townsend's Warbler © Craig Kerns

© 2018 by Oliver James
First paperback edition, 2023

The Library of Congress has cataloged the original 2018 edition as follows:

Names: James, Oliver, 1991- author.
Title: Birds of Berkeley / Oliver James.
Description: Berkeley, California : Heyday, [2018] | Includes bibliographical
    references.
Identifiers: LCCN 2017043201| ISBN 9781597144070 (hardcover : alk. paper) |
    ISBN 9781597144520 (ebook)
Subjects: LCSH: Birds--California--Berkeley.
Classification: LCC QL684.C2 J36 2018 | DDC 598.09794/67--dc23
LC record available at https://lccn.loc.gov/2017043201

Cover Art: California Scrub Jay (front) and Anna's Hummingbird (back) by
    Oliver James
Cover Design: Marlon Rigel
Interior Design/Typesetting: Ashley Ingram and Oliver James

Published by Heyday
P.O. Box 9145, Berkeley, California 94709
(510) 549-3564
heydaybooks.com

Printed in East Peoria, Illinios, by Versa Press, Inc.

10 9 8 7 6 5 4 3 2 1

Once again, to Rich Stallcup

The Pirate of Point Reyes

1944–2012

I hope you love birds too. It is economical.

It saves going to heaven.

—Emily Dickinson

CONTENTS

AUTHOR'S NOTE

"It is the province of this work to appreciate and, so far as it is possible, to express, not alone the conceptual entities of science called species, but the very persons and lives of those hundreds of millions of our fellow travelers and sojourners called birds."
—William Leon Dawson, *The Birds of California*

Back on inauguration day, January 20, 2017, as the maelstrom of punditry reached its crescendo, the Ecology Center here in Berkeley posted a short entry to its blog, dusting off an old truism: positive change has, and always will, begin at the community level, regardless of who's in office. *Recommit to those around you.*

We live in a society that slumps toward placelessness and namelessness. The Dakota Access Pipeline is rerouted from Bismarck to land that is ostensibly valueless. Our bombs, as if bombs were somehow discerning, fall only over terrorists; over countries that, ironically, we cannot recall. Closer to home, we repeat these names, lest their lives cease to matter: Jordan Edwards, Alton Sterling, Alejandro Nieto, Oscar Grant...

In a system that peddles anonymity, the work of resistance begins by becoming a student of place—its history, its people, its ecology. If, for you, local familiarity extends merely to the vegetables in your CSA box, think again. How about antigentrification activism, labor organizing, community banking and energy systems, antiracism training? Each is sown in the same soil. Buying organic is good; knowing your farmer is better. Prioritize real relationships.

So why natural history, and why now? Here's the answer that, I believe, matters most today: Whether it's flowers or fish, mushrooms or mammals, the study of natural history grounds us firmly in time and place. *What is the average arrival date of a Wilson's Warbler in Berkeley? Is it getting earlier? What's that type of tree it's nesting in? Are its fruits edible?* Birds act as a biological clock and litmus test for community ecological health. It is impossible to observe one slice of life and ignore the rest. The study of birds hones empathy.

As I write this, we've just closed out the hottest year in recorded history—again—and the water is still not safe to drink in Flint, Michigan. Since 1980, the black community in Berkeley has decreased by half. We will need to break through our anonymity to confront these problems. So get out into your city. Comment at a city council meeting. Give your ears and eyes.

And while you're at it, learn twenty-five species of Berkeley birds, by sight, by sound, by heart. I challenge you. May you reap the rewards of this work.

See you in the streets, in the field.

OLIVER JAMES
Berkeley, CA
Spring 2017

INTRODUCTION

PRESENTATION AND ORGANIZATION

This field guide is for a specific audience: the people of Berkeley. In the following pages, I introduce twenty-five fellow citizens, some of the most familiar birds that live, work, and play here. Although this book should be useful as an introduction to the birds of the Bay Area in general, that is not the express intention of this guide. This book focuses on birds regularly found within the city of Berkeley, more or less proper. My choice to feature these particular twenty-five neighbors over others is, of course, a subjective decision. This guide is not comprehensive, as there are upwards of one hundred other species that regularly frequent our city and can be located without much effort.

This book features original colored-pencil illustrations. It will be immediately apparent that they diverge from the traditional field guide format. Most contemporary scientific illustrators, to prioritize practicality, present their subjects lined up in profile, shoulder to shoulder across the page as if they are soldiers at attention, ten-hut. The result is more archetypal than animate, and that's exactly what is required for identification on the fly. Anyone who's ever picked up a Peterson, a Sibley, a Hansen, or a Laws appreciates just how lucky we are to have these incredible tomes. When your goal is field-preparedness, to be equipped to solve any identification thrown at you, these are the all-stars you want on your team.

I'm pursuing a different vision with my compositional choices. This guide privileges relationships, to place and to populace. I remain committed to scientific accuracy, but positive identification, after all, is just the first date. I attempt to depict each bird in a way that captures the physicality and personality unique to each species, qualities often overlooked as useful field marks and some of the most rewarding aspects of patient wildlife observation. (You can identify a good friend from a thousand paces just by the way they walk. Same with birds.) The trade-off: not every feather is visible in these pages. Remember that each individual bird in the field will never be identical to another of its same species. Depending on age, sex, subspecies, range, life history, or the time of year of observation, each will display different field marks, subtly or strikingly so. For instance, many species are sexually dimorphic: plumage, body size and proportion, and behavior differ between the sexes. Furthermore, juvenile and immature plumages often differ dramatically from those of an adult. True to the creative vision of this book, this field guide does not attempt to load you with all this intraspecific variation. May this book be the appetizer that sparks a lifelong study.

Each species account features an individual that is fairly representative of the community unique to our city. I highlight the field marks essential to the identification of this bird in the accompanying text, whether or not those field marks are visible in my illustration. When a species is strongly dimorphic, I describe the opposite sex. I do not describe juvenile birds (in the majority of cases).

On a final note, the birds in a field guide are typically organized taxonomically. Berkeley has a habit of bucking worn-out cultural mores: in this field guide, I introduce your neighbors in no particular order.

COMMON NAME

SCIENTIFIC NAME ─┐

GOLDEN-CROWNED SPARROW

TIME OF YEAR WHEN PRESENT

Zonotrichia atricapilla ─┘

L 7.25" ─┐

SPECIES ACCOUNT

September to May

As if by listener request, just as the afternoon shadows start to lengthen, the Golden-crowned Sparrows arrive with the mood music. Fresh off the tundra, the rush of the breeding season lingers on their vocal chords. It's a melancholy, three-note soundtrack that descends with the fleeting light. Some days, two notes are all they can muster.

The Bay Area is often mocked for its unusual calendar. Winter is a pushover, they say. Spring, unearned, unfolds in January, spoiling us until summer pulls its flaxen blanket across the landscape—and we pull on our July sweaters. Hardly a color riot, fall is more back-to-school convention than hemispheric revolution. Critics object to a seasonal arrhythmia.

So what, our calendar is no twelve-bar blues. The downbeat is still right there, listen: the music of the Golden-crowned Sparrow, like the plangent calls of geese, is perfectly scored to the tilting of the earth. They sing of the crunch of dry leaves and the impermanence of all things.

TOTAL LENGTH (TIP OF BEAK TO TAIL)

IDENTIFICATION

Brown crown stripes with a yellowish forehead. Gray-brown overall. Similar in appearance to White-crowned Sparrow, with which it is often found in mixed flocks.

VOICE

Occasionally gives song, or a fragment thereof: three (or only two) clear, descending whistles, *oh dear me*. By the end of the year, mostly silent.

DESCRIPTION OF PRIMARY VOCALIZATIONS

DESCRIPTION OF ESSENTIAL FIELD MARKS

BIRD TOPOGRAPHY

It is useful to have a specific, common vocabulary to describe the parts of a bird when sorting out identification.

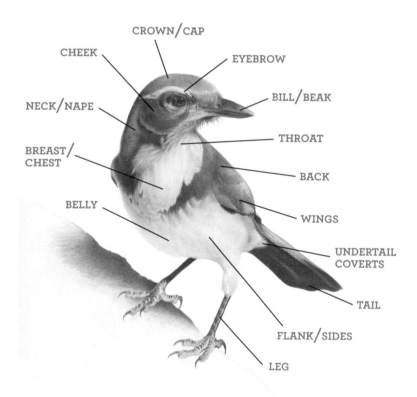

CROWN/CAP

CHEEK

EYEBROW

NECK/NAPE

BILL/BEAK

THROAT

BREAST/
CHEST

BACK

BELLY

WINGS

UNDERTAIL
COVERTS

TAIL

FLANK/SIDES

LEG

Songs vs. calls: In lay terms, songs are the vocalizations made by birds that are diagnostically melodious. Typically, calls are briefer, more simple musically, and not broadcasted in the same manner. Scientifically, calls and songs are differentiated by function. Songs are related to sexual behavior: to attract mates and declare territorial boundaries. They are usually produced by males (and sometimes females), in the breeding season (but not exclusively). Calls can convey information about relative location between pairs or groups and the presence of food or danger. Typically, birds have many calls but only one primary song. Nota bene: Not all birds sing. Birds, like humans, also have discernible dialects.

Molt: For birds, molting is the process of dropping and replacing feathers. Almost all birds molt all their feathers at least once a year. The pattern of molt, however, is extremely variable depending on species, age, time of year, and individual. For experienced birders, unique molt patterns can be supplemental identification tools. In the majority of cases, a bird is readily identifiable without considering molt; however, it is useful to have a basic understanding. There are three primary nomenclatures used to describe molt cycles. Two are found in this book. The most familiar is the breeding/nonbreeding (summer/winter) binary. This system serves well for descriptive purposes; it is, however, not technically precise and may not always correspond to molt. The other system referred to in these pages is the "life-year system," which references the calendar age of the bird, just as we do for humans.

SOME BRIEF ADVICE ON APPROACHING
BIRD IDENTIFICATION

Identifying birds in the field is, by definition, hard. Here are some useful tips to carry around in your vest pocket:

Ask yourself, is this reasonable? Let's say I'm looking at a red finch that I suspect is a Red Crossbill. Am I in the expected range and habitat for this species? Is it the right time of year? What do I know about the bird's expected behavior? Its vocalizations? Basically, why is this red finch in my yard *not* a House Finch or a Purple Finch, which are more expected? Increase your batting average by approaching identification holistically and conservatively.

Light and shadow play tricks. There's a reason why artists are so fussy about lighting: our eyes are not perfectly reliable instruments. A bird seen in the shade can magically transform as it steps out into the light. Beware: judging the relative size of birds in different spectral environments, especially when silhouetted, is notoriously inconsistent.

Your mind can play tricks. Every (honest) birder has a story to share: the thrill of the chase can lead one to anticipate discoveries, even field marks that are not actually there. Recalling field marks in hindsight is especially unreliable. Taking timely field notes is a good habit.

Auditory cues are your secret weapon. Learning how to identify birds by sound is one of the most useful and rewarding arrows you can add to your quiver. For many of us, our ears can cast a much wider and finer net than our eyes. Small birds, often the most cryptic to identify, are frequently the most loquacious! There are lots of good digital resources online to train with prior to heading out into the field.

Good optics make a BIG difference. Birds can be shy even around the most patient observer. Investing in a good pair of binoculars can make a world of difference in easing identification and bringing to life the nuanced field marks and subtle body language of a bird. Too often beginning birders struggle with poor optics and grow frustrated by learning the ropes. If you are serious about wildlife observation, consider investing in a decent pair of binoculars.

SPECIES

RED-BREASTED NUTHATCH
Sitta canadensis
L 4.5"
Year Round

Red-breasted Nuthatches are round, fluffy birds that get swallowed up in the dense needles of tall conifer trees, fully absorbed in their work. Picture a team of miniature arboreal manicurists meticulously grooming a tree of insects to a heigh-ho tune of tiny tin trumpets. They leave no crease of bark unexamined, no fold or flake of skin untouched, pampering acrobatically up and down each and every limb. The tree is left feeling radiant.

This is a good example of an "irruptive" species—a bird that, depending on cone production in the boreal heartland of its breeding range, may be forced to lower latitudes to ride out the long winter. Some years, nuthatches are everywhere in our area, and other years they are nearly absent.

The last major irruption occurred during the winter of 2012. From Berkeley to Baton Rouge, New Year's Day 2013 arrived with a fanfare of tiny taps. The Red-breasted Nuthatch is not quite the Miles Davis of bird land—critics invoke the sound of reversing trucks as a musical influence—and yet, practice makes perfect. What it lacks in improvisational flair, it more than makes up in diligence.

IDENTIFICATION
Plump body with stubby wings and tail. Dark eye-line and white eyebrow. Rusty orange underparts and plain blue-gray above. Acrobatic, tree-hugging foraging behavior distinctive.

VOICE
Nasal, excitable *yank yank yank,* often repeated incessantly.

RUBY-CROWNED KINGLET

Regulus calendula
L 4.25"
September to April

Physical traits—color and shape—are often the most salient field marks used in identification. But what if we encounter a bird that shares a very similar paint job and body type with other birds on the lot? Take the decals off a stock, olive-green Chrysler 300 and it looks surprisingly like a luxe, olive-green Bentley. How do we spot the knockoff?

As in cars, so in birds: the difference is under the hood.

The Ruby-crowned Kinglet is a classic test. A common winter visitor to the Bay Area, this bird can blend surprisingly well into the local crowd and has an uncanny doppelganger in the Hutton's Vireo. Put the vireo and the kinglet head-to-head on the road and the resemblance falls away. The kinglet is frantic through the turns, constantly flicking its wings and hovering nimbly to glean insects from beneath leaves. Redline this ride and the bird raises its crown feathers, exposing its crimson racing stripe. Now get behind the wheel of the vireo: Feel the difference? Its slower acceleration; its methodical pace?

Consumer Reports (or your Sibley guide) is a great place to start when you're a new buyer (or birder). But before you sign the lease on that ID, take it for a test drive: behavior is just as important as color and shape.

IDENTIFICATION
Olive-green body with small, thin bill. White ring around eye. White bar adjacent to black bar across folding wing. Beware: the ruby-red crown of the male is visible only in moments of serious road rage (i.e., territorial disputes).

VOICE
Call is most often heard in Berkeley: husky, staccato *jidit,* often repeated. Snippets of the male's long, lively song overheard occasionally, but normally sung on the breeding ground.

CEDAR WAXWING

Bombycilla cedrorum
L 7.25"
August to May

Waxwings return with the Cal students, crossing the threshold of campus in small groups of party-goers carried south on a pulse of expectant energy. Come fall, the air is alive with their high, thin whistles.

Just in time for Rush Week, these eager pledges flock to the fruiting ornamentals along Fraternity Row in feathered dresses and manicured wing tips, each jockeying to stand out from the crowd. The rabble spills out into the streets at last call, bellies full of fermenting berries, swallowed whole; kohl slashed across their faces, a Winehouse homage. Not everyone will make it home safely: waxwings are known for an alarming trend of DUI window collisions.

Through football tailgates and Cal Day festivities, these snowbirds indulge in our local brew for the entire academic calendar. Come June, however, the door slams on the last northbound convertible, high heels and dress shirts stuffed hastily into luggage. Long summer days beckon at higher latitudes.

IDENTIFICATION
Like freshmen, almost always in found in loose flocks, some quite large. While in Berkeley, feed almost exclusively on berries, occasionally becoming intoxicated when the fruit is overripe. Warm brown head and chest, yellowish belly. Gray wings and tail with a yellow tip. Black mask across the face. Loose pompadour.

VOICE
Call is a very high, thin whistle, often difficult to detect for the hard of hearing.

WESTERN GULL
Larus occidentalis
L 25"
Year Round

In birding school, gull identification is like an asinine word problem or long-division worksheet: the typical reaction is to groan, flip to the answer in the back of the textbook, and then move on to something else. Before settling into a familiar adult plumage, a young gull changes costumes like a runway model. Worse, gulls regularly hybridize; like Schrödinger's Cat, they defy logical categorization. It's enough to make your head hurt.

Most of the Western Gulls found at the Berkeley waterfront were likely born on Southeast Farallon Island, thirty miles west of the Golden Gate, where the highly productive California Current supports about 30 percent of the global population. Despite the local, organic options, however, gulls, like us, have guilty pleasures. Satellite tags reveal that some adults commute all the way from the Farallons to the dumpsters behind Oracle Arena to pick up chicken nuggets for the kids.

If you encounter folks with binoculars loafing in said smelly places, don't be confused. Those whom we call nerds call themselves Larophiles ("gull lovers"). These Poindexters frequent the city dump by day and debate the minutiae of molt patterns in esoteric chat rooms by night—and typically wind up at NASA or in the Birding Hall of Fame.

So, kids, do your math homework.

IDENTIFICATION
Requires patience. A fourth-calendar-year, breeding-plumaged adult is pictured here. Note the thick, yellow bill with a red spot, dusky iris, and yellow-orange ring around eye. Adults have charcoal-gray backs, white underparts, black wing tips, and pink legs.

VOICE
Loud, clear cries, often chanted.

CHESTNUT-BACKED CHICKADEE
Poecile rufescens
L 4.75"
Year Round

Though hard to comprehend, there was a time, not too long ago, when Chestnut-backed Chickadees were big news in Berkeley. Their distribution, up until the 1940s, encompassed the cool, woody coastal ranges from San Luis Obispo County all the way to Alaska—with one conspicuous gap. Despite favorable habitat, the East Bay was empty space on the map, and here's why: chickadees love trees.

They are so partial to them, in fact, that wide, tree-less areas pose a physical barrier. To the south, chickadees in Santa Cruz were reluctant to cross the Santa Clara Valley, historically a vast system of marshes and oak savannah; to the north, chickadees in Sebastopol were averse to fording the Sacramento–San Joaquin Delta; and for another distinct population in Marin County, crossing the San Francisco Bay was sacrilege. For hundreds of years, these isolated tribes waited on opposite ends of a big moat, staring across at the Berkeley hills floating like an island in no-man's-land—until the maturation of orchards and shade trees, planted by humans, unlocked a southern passage.

We are good at burning bridges and building them. Berkeley is no longer an island: the first chickadee pioneer (of the southern subspecies *barlowi*) was recorded nesting on the UC Berkeley campus in the spring of 1950. Today they are ubiquitous.

IDENTIFICATION
Bold white cheeks contrasting with a black cap and bib. Chestnut back. Gray-brown flanks.

VOICE
Most familiar call is a husky *chick-a-dee,* the *dee* often repeated one or more times; says its name.

ANNA'S HUMMINGBIRD
Calypte anna
L 4"
Year Round

In the spring, male hummingbirds find conspicuous perches to parade their superhuman abilities. Hovering just out of reach like the golden snitch, these champions can fly backwards or ascend straight up into the firmament, feats no other bird is capable of. Their feathery costumes, as if cut from the sublime cloth of the X-Men suits, empower them to bend light and summon music from the wind:

[To be read in the manner of the breaking newscaster] Having stunned a prospective female with a blinding flash from his pink gorget, our tiny hero rockets straight up into the sky, only to plunge back to earth in a meteoric dive. At the last second he pulls up, the air surging through his specialized tail feathers, releasing an explosive (if proportionately sized) sonic boom. The crowd erupts below.

Every male hummingbird, by species, rolls out his signature display, unique in shape and sound. Look for male Anna's Hummingbirds fighting crime and performing their J-shaped dives anywhere in the vicinity of ornamental plants. Like Superman's need for solar energy, a hummingbird requires flower power.

IDENTIFICATION
Male (pictured here) has iridescent pink gorget that covers throat and crown; female just a few pink throat feathers. Note that these feathers refract pink light; if ground up, they would become gray dust. Upperparts iridescent green and underparts dingy gray-green.

VOICE
Song is a a roughly eight-second series of unmelodic, scratchy buzzes; may not register as birdsong. At the end of their courtship dives, males produce a loud squeak, once thought to be another type of call, now known to originate from air rushing over their modified outer tail feathers.

CALIFORNIA SCRUB JAY

Aphelocoma californica
L 11.5"
Year Round

It seems reasonable to assume that science has compiled a fairly complete catalog of life on Earth. With millions of observers wielding millions of GoPros, what could possibly have evaded our detection until now? Surprisingly much: In 2014, a giant, carnivorous plant was newly described in Brazil after a picture of it was discovered on Facebook. On average, 18,000 new species are described each year (though the math is disputed). No need to plumb the Mariana Trench; new species are hiding in plain sight. Allow me to introduce you to one of them. It's in your backyard.

In 2016, the Western Scrub Jay monopoly was dissolved, recognizing two distinct species where once there was one. Despite superficial similarity, the bright azure individuals loyal to Berkeley and the Pacific seaboard, now called California Scrub Jays, rarely interbreed with the steel-blue birds of the interior West, justifying a split. Both populations are distinct from yet a third, the Island Scrub Jay, cobalt behemoth of Santa Cruz Island, a product of prior antitrust action. Collect all three! California is the only participating retailer.

What else have we overlooked in our city, on Planet Earth?

IDENTIFICATION
Bright azure head, necklace, tail, and wings. Back is gray-brown. White underparts.

VOICE
Most familiar call is a rising *shreeenk,* loud and harsh.

WRENTIT
Chamaea fasciata
L 6.5"
Year Round

Everyone is good at something. In 2016, the Arctic Tern reclaimed the world ultramarathon title by pulling off sixty thousand miles in a year, knocking out the rangy Sooty Shearwater. Multiplied over a lifetime (this is an annual journey, mind you), the champion will travel nearly 1.8 *million* miles, four round-trips to the moon.

The Wrentit is not a distance specialist. Over its own lifetime, a Wrentit successfully ventures about a half mile from its birthplace, maybe less, earning its unassailable reputation as the Most Sedentary Bird in America. Alongside the feats of Neil Armstrong and Amelia Earhart, it is, perhaps, one of the great distinctions in aviation history.

Call it good genes: The Wrentit pedigree has baffled geneticists for decades. As if dropped off from some other planet, this peculiar bird claims no obvious earthly relatives, thrown in for now with a distant family in East Asia. Nonetheless, a Wrentit is never lonely. The grandkids will leave home soon and move two doors down the block. (There's been grousing over millennials and the death of the Empty Nest.)

IDENTIFICATION
Plain brownish overall with a piercing pale iris. Long tailed and short billed. Usually very cryptic—best detected by voice.

VOICE
Song is an accelerating series of short whistles, compared to a bouncing ball. Call is a dry, scolding *trrk*.

EUROPEAN STARLING
Sturnus vulgaris
L 8.5"
Year Round

The curtain rises on our tragic hero Eugene Schieffelin, chairman of the American Acclimatization Society, as he unloads birdcages from a horse-drawn carriage in Central Park, Manhattan. The year is 1890 and the electronic cacophony of starlings fills the air.

Schieffelin, who chairs an organization committed to naturalizing European flora and fauna in America, largely for nostalgic purposes, is also an ardent Shakespeare buff. In true tragicomic form, he's hatched a plan that will be his undoing: release all the bird species mentioned by the Bard into the New World. Zoological colonialism is in fashion (he's already released Skylarks, Nightingales, Chaffinches, and House Sparrows, to name a few); environmental impact statements not so much.

Alas, all that glitters is not gold! When our tragic hero looses the starlings (see *Henry IV, Part 1*) he unwittingly uncorks one of the most notorious continental invasions since the arrival of the *Mayflower*. By 1949, having overrun the entire country, trailing ecological and agricultural disruption in their wake, starlings march on the Bay Area, some three thousand miles away. We will remain under occupation for the foreseeable future.

IDENTIFICATION
Breeding adult (pictured here) is iridescent purple and green (in poor light appears black) with some pale spots and a bright yellow bill. Nonbreeding adult is duller, more boldly spotted, and has a dark bill.

VOICE
Song is an electronic, gurgling chatter that often includes imitations of other birds' vocalizations.

FORSTER'S TERN

Sterna forsteri
L 13"
Year Round

The game of birding can be played nearly anywhere, anytime: How many different species can you find in your yard? From your office window? In your county? (As of press time, the twenty-four-hour record in Alameda County is 172. In a year? 267.)

One of the best times to bird is during rush hour. When traffic is inching along the 880 straightaway, only one hand is needed at the wheel. With your free hand on your binoculars and an hour to kill between the Ashby and University exits, can you break thirty? An armada of Greater Scaup (one) marshals offshore of Frontage Road while a Forster's Tern (two) fishes nimbly overhead, landing more fingerling Topsmelt per minute than you're moving in feet.

On a less enthusiastic note, because of their piscatorial diet, Forster's Terns bioaccumulate environmental toxins. The population in the Bay Area claims a notorious title: their eggs contain the highest levels of PBDEs, a hormone disruptor used in flame retardants, of any other bird tested anywhere in the world. Mercury, a legacy of gold mining in the state, is also of concern: within two months of arriving to breed in the Bay Area, the terns' blood mercury levels increase threefold.

IDENTIFICATION
Breeding adult (pictured here) white overall with a black crown. Black tip to an orange bill. On nonbreeding birds, the black crown is replaced by a black eye patch and an all-dark bill. Often seen foraging back and forth over open water, diving frequently, terns have slender, swept-back wings and a distinct buoyant flight.

VOICE
Call is a lively, descending *keerrr*.

WHITE-CROWNED SPARROW

Zonotrichia leucophrys
L 7"
Year Round

If you live in midcoastal California, you associate these things with home: fog, summer tourists shivering in tank tops, and the song of the White-crowned Sparrow. White-crowned Sparrows come in five flavors, four of which are migratory. The fifth, the Nuttall's subspecies, faithfully abides in the long sliver of the so-called coastal "fog belt," from southern Humboldt to Santa Barbara Counties. This is a hard rule: no fog, no Nuttall's.

Along an otherwise durable seaside levee, there exists, however, a spectacular fault. Like clockwork, in summer, the misty tidal wave strikes once a day: rushing through the wide mouth of the Golden Gate, the swirling comber topples the Sutro Tower and crashes into the Campanile like a lighthouse, finally burning off as it crests the ridge at the head of Strawberry Canyon.

And there, at the high-water mark, anchored to the same Coyote Bush where it was born, is a Nuttall's White-crowned Sparrow, singing its small heart out like a tiny foghorn, the vanguard of a dwindling East Bay population (see Notes) relatively far from the mighty Pacific.

What lies beyond is fogless *terra incognita*. There are no Nuttall's White-crowned Sparrows in Orinda.

IDENTIFICATION
Adult (pictured here) has bold black and white crown stripes; first-winter birds have brown and tan crown stripes. Yellow bill. Gray-brown overall.

VOICE
Dialects vary mile by mile; a bird at the Berkeley Marina sings a slightly different song than a bird at Point Isabel than a bird in Golden Gate Park. The general form: two clear whistles followed by a descending trill of buzzy whistles.

COOPER'S HAWK
Accipiter cooperii
L 16.5"
Year Round

Unlike a broad-winged raptor that soars around in the heavens drone-like before falling out of the sky, Cooper's Hawks are built for white-knuckle pursuits through trees. Imagine Steve McQueen in a '68 Mustang, and you, the pigeon, in a rental car with a poor turning radius. You're fleeing down San Pablo Avenue, weaving through traffic. It's all over in a matter of seconds.

Cooper's Hawks live in Berkeley in one of the highest densities known in an urban area (approximately one pair per square mile, according to the Golden Gate Raptor Observatory). Unlike the human housing market, raptor real estate in the East Bay is plentiful, safe, and affordable—a mature tree in Codornices Park akin to a rent-controlled Fifth Avenue penthouse suite.

Sadly, urban living does come at a cost: rat poisons, despite widespread collateral damage to wildlife, pets, and people, are still available over the counter. These rodenticides accumulate in the food chain, paradoxically wiping out the most cost-effective pest-control technology available: *raptors*. Berkeley's Coops are no exception; the Golden Gate Raptor Observatory has documented fatal poisonings of Cooper's Hawks every year since their study began.

IDENTIFICATION
Adults are steel-gray above with burnt-orange barring across white underparts. Dark bands across tail. Immature (pictured here) is brown above with dense, crisp streaking across the breast and neck. Most reliably differentiated from the Sharp-shinned Hawk by shape: in flight, head projects past leading edge of wings, with a long, attenuated tail —a "flying cross."

VOICE
Call is a chanted series of sharp, nasal notes, *kek-kek-kek-kek*, most often heard near nest site.

GOLDEN-CROWNED SPARROW

Zonotrichia atricapilla
L 7.25"
September to May

As if by listener request, just as the afternoon shadows start to lengthen, the Golden-crowned Sparrows arrive with the mood music. Fresh off the tundra, the rush of the breeding season lingers on their vocal chords. It's a melancholy, three-note soundtrack that descends with the fleeting light. Some days, two notes are all they can muster.

The Bay Area is often mocked for its unusual calendar. Winter is a pushover, they say. Spring, unearned, unfolds in January, spoiling us until summer pulls its flaxen blanket across the landscape—and we pull on our July sweaters. Hardly a color riot, fall is more back-to-school convention than hemispheric revolution. Critics object to a seasonal arrhythmia.

So what, our calendar is no twelve-bar blues. The downbeat is still right there, listen: the music of the Golden-crowned Sparrow, like the plangent calls of geese, is perfectly scored to the tilting of the earth. They sing of the crunch of dry leaves and the impermanence of all things.

IDENTIFICATION
Brown crown stripes with a yellowish forehead. Gray-brown overall. Similar in appearance to White-crowned Sparrow, with which it is often found in mixed flocks.

VOICE
Occasionally gives song, or a fragment thereof: three (or only two) clear, descending whistles, *oh dear me*. By the end of the year, mostly silent.

HERMIT THRUSH

Catharus guttatus
L 6.75"
September to June

The thrush occupies a special place in poetry. Known for its beautiful music, the thrush, to the Romantic poets of England, was a herald of hope, its song rising impromptu from the depths of winter's icy cage. In the American canon, the allegorical thrush inhabits a different lyrical habitat, its music rarely "heard" on the vernal equinox.

While poet Mary Oliver's thrush shares similar genes with Keats's, these poets are describing different species, with one operative distinction: thrushes in New England are migratory. On March 21, while Keats's Mistle Thrush is thawing out the hearts of mankind under the "frozen stars," Oliver's Wood Thrush is still vacationing in the Panamanian jungle. Due to its itinerary, Oliver's thrush rarely sings, in life or in stanza, when there's fresh snow on the ground. She instead likens her transient herald to "Verdi or Mahler," a thrilling musician that, if heard "every day, all day," would "exhaust anyone"—a messenger with a slightly different memo.

A breeder in high-elevation alpine forests, the Hermit Thrush sings an ethereal song rarely heard in our neck of the woods. Look for this thrush instead at the end of the year, in that corner of your yard where the undergrowth is damp and dark: with a nod to the Romantics, they will emerge from the shadows where the light cannot reach.

IDENTIFICATION
Warm brown above and white below with bold black spots through the breast. Distinct, rust-colored tail. Stands with proper singing posture, bill tipped up.

VOICE
Song is rarely heard in Berkeley proper: ethereal, flute-like. Call is a soft, low *chup.*

BUSHTIT

Psaltriparus minimus
L 4.5"
Year Round

These bite-sized birds spend most of the year in boisterous flocks, meandering through wooded areas. Like a snowball rolling downhill, a flock of bushtits tends to absorb nearby birds as it goes. Small birds, like chickadees, kinglets, and warblers, get sucked up into its gravitational field, and eventually you have a ravenous planetary body hurtling around the neighborhood.

Bushtits may be small, but they are master builders. Using spiderwebs and plant materials, they weave a nest like a Christmas stocking that sways up to a foot below its anchor point. The visionary architecture is matched by a progressive social behavior within: at odds with normative gender roles, a mated pair may receive regular child-rearing support gratis from neighbors, especially from local bachelors. (This behavior is rare in our area, however.)

Because of their high surface area–to–body mass ratio, Bushtits are not energy efficient, so they bunk together, packed like fluffy sardines to conserve body heat. Batteries recharged overnight, the gang hits the pavement at dawn, rearing to eat their way through the city—80 percent of their weight in insects. Yield to emergency vehicles: when Bushtits are hangry, they always have the right of way.

IDENTIFICATION
Tiny, gray-brown cotton-ball-with-a-tail, almost always found in lively flocks. Males have dark iris; females pale.

VOICE
Chorus of tinkling *chip* notes; loose change jingling in a pocket.

CALIFORNIA TOWHEE

Melozone crissalis
L 9"
Year Round

The California Towhee may be the most Berkeley bird of them all. And no, this is not because of veganism or lefty activist tendencies—it espouses neither. Rather, in most years, out of 1,800 censuses across the country, the Oakland Christmas Bird Count (in which Berkeley is included) records the highest number of California Towhees of all. Go ahead Angeleños, tout your dubious claim as the Doughnut Capital; the East Bay is the *undisputed* California Towhee Capital of the World.

Right at home in the Mediterranean climate of coastal Californian cities, California Towhees are year-round residents in Berkeley and one of the city's original families. Like their great-great-great grandparents before them, the fledglings will enter the sixth grade this year at Willard Middle School. Their textbooks still neglect this detail however: Towhees occupied People's Park long before the National Guard showed up.

What for us is a pedestrian sight—as common as tie-dye on Telegraph—is a sought-after species by birders from across the country, a near endemic to our state. Currently, the California Quail is our official state bird, a bird found natively in at least six other states and provinces. Nothing personal against the bumbling quail, but perhaps it's time to fly our true colors.

IDENTIFICATION
Matte brown overall with cinnamon undertail coverts and markings through the face. Often found hopping along the ground.

VOICE
Call is most often heard: a single, loud, metallic *pink*. Song is a series of these notes uttered together in a short, accelerating trill.

WESTERN MEADOWLARK
Sturnella neglecta
L 9.5"
September to April

Pre-Depression Berkeley was a time of unconstrained expansion: (whites-only) neighborhoods popped up overnight—Northbrae, Claremont, Elmwood, Thousand Oaks—as streetcar lines pushed out beyond city limits. Maybeck and Morgan were busy cementing the foundation of their legacy. In 1908, the State Capital was nearly relocated here.

And yet, despite all this growth, the city retained field marks of its rural past. "The [Berkeley] hills from a distance look bare and untimbered," reported Joseph Grinnell in his 1914 edition of the "List of the Birds of the Berkeley Campus." From a bald Vollmer Peak, grassy slopes coursed through glen and draw down into town, where the morning cry of the Key Route conductor mingled with that of the Rufous-crowned Sparrow, today both silent. After a century of suburbanization and habitat loss, this landscape has transformed—the dawn chorus, too.

Among a host of birds once listed by Grinnell as "common," the decline of one in particular ushered in a ringing silence:

It is said that in the early 1900s, a sea of meadowlarks "three miles wide" spanned the bare hills between Berkeley and Oakland. Every morning, as workers assembled at the Shattuck Avenue line, bound for the Emeryville Ferry and on to San Francisco, a spring symphony of meadowlarks, liquid and powerful, rained down upon the city. Today the sun is greeted by the whisper of electric cars.

IDENTIFICATION
Bright yellow underparts with a black V across the breast (these colors fade in fall and winter). Upperparts intricately patterned brown. White outer tail feathers flash in flight.

VOICE
Male's song is rich and gurgling. Starts with a few clear whistles and ends with a descending warble. Carries over vast distances.

TOWNSEND'S WARBLER

Setophaga townsendi
L 5"
August to May

Warblers are the precious gemstones of the bird world; like discovering a glistening sliver of obsidian, spotting a warbler activates some deep, involuntary reaction: Glittering up in the canopy, a warbler seduces you off the trail and into the forest, neck craned as you stumble over roots and rocks. Before you realize it, you're wading through a creek or lowering yourself over a cliff to identify this twinkling treasure.

Every spring, especially in eastern states, which claim higher warbler diversity than those out west, birders flock to national warbler festivals like about-face forty-niners hoping to strike it rich. It is not uncommon to line one's checklist with upward of twenty-five warbler species in a day, in every shade of jade, opal, and citrine. Back at the hotel, the lucky prospectors parade their booty across T-shirts and tote bags.

The Townsend's Warbler, known for its elemental glow, is one of the most prized talismans of the West. A breeder in the cool, coniferous forests to our north, it is a winter visitor to Berkeley. Focus your search in the scattered redwoods and pines around the city: with a little luck, you are bound to strike it rich.

IDENTIFICATION

Male (pictured here) has striking black throat, crown, cheeks, and flank streaking against lemon-yellow face, breast, and sides. Olive-green back. Two white bars across folded wing. On female, cheek and crown olive-green; black limited to throat.

VOICE

Only sings on breeding ground (i.e., not in Berkeley). Call is a sharp *tsik* that can be distinguished from that of other warblers with careful practice.

BLACK PHOEBE

Sayornis nigricans
L 7"
Year Round

Hindu gods are inextricably linked with particular *vahanas,* animals that serve as vehicles to carry and extend their corresponding deities, both physically and metaphysically. Captured within each animal-deity pairing is a symbolic dualism: the traits of the animal serve as a reminder of the divine.

The Black Phoebe has an affinity for water. Any body of water will do: Lake Anza, the Marin Circle fountain, even a kiddie pool. For an experienced birder, the soft call of a Black Phoebe immediately evokes its preferred habitat. Exploring the boardwalk trail in the Tilden Nature Area, a well-trained ear would know, for instance, what awaits at the end (spoiler: Jewel Lake). Oracles studied augury for a reason: a dedicated naturalist can just about predict the future.

Perhaps the Black Phoebe is the *vahana* of some lesser god, a quiet deity that watches over small bodies of water. Nearing the final bend in the trail, the call of the bird, simple and earnest, heralds your arrival at Her altar.

IDENTIFICATION
Black head, breast, back, wings, and tail. White below belly. Often wags tail when perched.

VOICE
Song is a series of bright, two-syllable whistles, *tee-hee tee-hoo.* Call is an earnest, repeated *teer.*

OAK TITMOUSE
Baeolophus inornatus
L 5.75"
Year Round

Deciphering bird language is a hot topic these days. With the aid of spectrographic equipment, scientists are revealing how birds, with subtle shifts in pitch and tempo, convey information about the type, size, and location of danger. What's more, we've learned that birds of different species (as well as other animals) eavesdrop on one another—that the whole forest is tuned in—and that word travels very, very fast. It's nature's Twitter: everyone knows what the hawk had for breakfast before she's finished eating it.

With American journalism in decline, many woodland creatures have turned to titmice to get their news. When timely information is a matter of life or death, titmice cut through the clickbait; their Twitter feed reads like a police scanner typed #IN ALL CAPS (i.e., loud and clear). Birders take advantage of this social medium, too, when they use a vocal technique called "pishing," a raspy sound that loosely imitates the alarm calls of birds in the Paridae family, of which the Oak Titmouse is a member. So, yes: Pishing is the equivalent of trolling nature's Twittersphere with fake news. Feathers are ruffled, and pretty soon you've got a small riot in the comments section.

Even a shy bird comes out for a closer look.

IDENTIFICATION
Plain gray overall. Shaggy gray hairdo (often spiked). Spunky.

VOICE
Song is a series of varied, shrill whistled phrases. Chooses one at a time and repeats it over and over. Call is a series of rapid, hoarse, scolding notes.

AMERICAN ROBIN

Turdus migratorius
L 10"
Year Round

The excitement that surrounds recent discoveries in avian communication (some of which I just described) is warranted, but let's back up a second. In truth, scientists are *re*-discovering this fluency. Ask any student of "deep bird language," a modern English name for the bilingualism practiced by Native trackers for millennia: You don't need a PhD to translate what a bird is telling you. All you need is to pay supremely close attention.

We all overlook robins. Widespread and abundant, the American Robin blends into the prevailing landscape no matter where you go. There they are tugging on earthworms at the Gabe Catalfo soccer fields; there, too, plucking berries at the crest of the Sierra Nevada. Robins have quietly weathered many storms—DDT, for instance, which accumulates in earthworms—and still their song is the first to greet the day.

In a class of animals that has survived on this planet a lot longer than we have, the robin is a particularly hardy species. So let's tune in: bird language, perhaps the earliest language known to mankind, is buried in our synapses. We have a lot to learn from that red-breasted dinosaur stalking earthworms across the front lawn.

IDENTIFICATION
Male (pictured here) has a blackish head, yellow bill, rich orange underparts, and dark gray upperparts. The plumage of the female is more subdued.

VOICE
Song is a series of clear whistled phrases that rise and fall in pitch, often described as *cheerily, cheer up, cheer up, cheerily.*

SNOWY EGRET
Egretta thula
L 24"
Year Round

Like a samurai, a Snowy Egret's most deadly weapon is its mind. As she hunts, thoughts and temptations conspire to scuttle the warrior's poise, yet she does not take the bait. She knows from experience: the battle for breakfast is won before the first shot is fired. Her grit has been tested in a far greater conflict.

Fashion designers have always tried to capture the spirit of birds in their work, but for the milliners (hat designers) of the late nineteenth century, there was not a shred of irony in the expression "put a bird on it." Hundreds of thousands of bird parts—feathers, wings, even entire taxidermied birds—adorned opulent hats in cities across the Western Hemisphere, and the Snowy Egret's diaphanous plumes fetched the highest price of all, more so than their weight in gold. Extinction reared its ugly head.

Nevertheless, she persisted: a group of women, torchbearers of the young National Audubon Society, mounted a heroic eleventh-hour campaign, securing passage of the Migratory Bird Treaty Act in 1918—a feather in the cap (restored to its native head). Today, it is unlawful to harm or take any native bird, and the egret population has rebounded.

IDENTIFICATION
Snow-white overall. Breeding adult displays lacy plumes from neck and back. Black bill and legs. Golden slippers.

VOICE
Mostly silent. Gives raspy calls at nesting site.

BURROWING OWL

Athene cunicularia
L 9.5"
October to March

What was once our city's dump, the Berkeley Marina today is a laboratory of upcycling. On one side of the street, children build castles out of reclaimed junk at the Adventure Playground while, on the other, adults have cleared away their rubble pile to make wildlife habitat. Birds find beauty in the margins: at high tide, cheeky Least Sandpipers eschew the man-made wetlands now and then to wade instead in the puddles that form in the dusty parking lot. One man's trash, as they say.

It's fitting that, year after year, one of Berkeley's most distinctive guests, in spite of vacancy at the Claremont Hotel, chooses to vacation here instead.

Every winter, Burrowing Owls, a California Species of Special Concern, sublet modest apartments from the portly ground squirrels in Cesar Chavez Park. Dug out from the riprap that fortifies our floating trash pile, they're either holes in the wall or bayfront cabanas, depending on your point of view. In any case, Burrowing Owls, drawn to in-between places, are an easy target of gentrification: the ones at the Marina are some of the last remaining Burrowing Owls in the East Bay.

IDENTIFICATION
Roosts in underground burrows—almost always found on or near the ground. Stands on tall legs. Barred undersides and spotted upperparts. White throat and eyebrows. Piercing yellow eyes.

VOICE
Song is a nasal *coo-coooo* on a constant pitch. Alarm call is a raspy, chattering *kwee-ch-ch-ch-ch*.

WESTERN SANDPIPER

Calidris mauri
L 6.5"
Year Round (August peak)

Born on the Yukon-Kuskokwim Delta, Alaska, on July 1, a Western Sandpiper walks away from the crib within hours but, hey, this is America: Mom and Dad get zero parental leave. Instead, a game of Battleship begins. To help it evade the Arctic Fox and Long-tailed Jaeger, natural selection chips in a simple safety net: the pattern of downy back feathers on a dime-sized chick uncannily mimics the pattern of prevailing tundra. Freeze and disappear.

On July 22, the survivors receive their pilot's licenses but Mom and Dad skip graduation. What follows is a bona fide world wonder.

It's August 20, and a caravan of adolescent sandpipers drops in at the mouth of Schoolhouse Creek in Berkeley. They've worked up a teenaged appetite: someway, somehow, these rookies have accomplished the 2,500-mile journey on their own—no practice test, no guidance counselor, no Google Maps. Meanwhile, hundreds of thousands of Western Sandpipers and other migratory shorebirds are piling into the San Francisco Bay, the largest rest stop on the conterminous Pacific coast. A jumpy feeling grips the crowd, a restlessness scientists call *zugunruhe*—perhaps a mere endocrinal instinct—or the sensation of knowing firsthand the audacity of life.

Bethlehem, the Golden Temple, the Ganges River, the San Francisco Bay: these are the destinations of the some of the world's great pilgrimages.

Black bill, long and slightly drooping (compared to that of the Least Sandpiper). By October, adults are in nonbreeding plumage: upperparts matte gray, underparts white. Come spring, they molt into breeding plumage: rufous feathers appear in the crown, cheek, and shoulders. Juvenile (pictured here) shows rufous shoulder feathers and warm tones in the crown and cheek.

VOICE
Flight call is a high, thin *cheet.*

BUFFLEHEAD

Bucephala albeola
L 13.5"
October to May

If you trace the original Berkeley shoreline by foot, part of your route will take you, more or less, down the meandering path on the east side of Aquatic Park. At high tide, the Bay creeps under twelve lanes of traffic into this man-made lagoon, a tiny simulacrum of what once was: Berkeley's flatlands, the terminus of five creeks, were once a lush floodplain, a land of Grizzly Bear, Tule Elk, and, according to early white settlers, flocks of waterfowl so dense as to block out the sun. Tall boots would have been necessary west of where Sixth Street is today.

With the onset of the Gold Rush, tons of industrial waste began accumulating in the Bay. Developers tasted blood: infill created something in shortage, waterfront property, an appetite so large that the City of Berkeley considered filling two thousand acres of open water in order to double in size. Thanks to Save the Bay and others, this plan was scrapped, but the momentum gained over a century would run its course. By 1961, the size of the San Francisco Bay had been reduced by a third.

As you wend your way through the disc golf course, Bufflehead dive offshore as if sifting for archaeological evidence. Local place names reveal some recent deposits: Brickyard Cove south of the Berkeley Marina and Battery Point north of Point Isabel. Other layers of history are not well advertised. If ducks could talk, they would describe traces of a towering Ohlone shellmound, older than the pyramids, among the hundreds of lost Frisbees.

IDENTIFICATION
Male (pictured here) is striking: a black forehead and back contrasting with clean white underparts, flanks, and back of head. Female is dark gray overall with a small white cheek patch.

VOICE
Generally silent.

ACKNOWLEDGMENTS

To my family: Carol Whaling for planting the seed; Ward and Marylou Whaling, John, Elizabeth, Bobbie, and Wendy James, David Herrick, Jeff Kerr, and Chris Bauer for watering it; my brother, Colin James, for putting up with family vacations hijacked to look for birds; and above all my parents, Anne Whaling and Christopher James, for your unending patience and dedication (and frequent rides to outer Point Reyes).

There are so many naturalist mentors who have touched my life, offering wisdom and guidance. In no particular order: Rich Stallcup, Alan Kaplan, Betsy Mitchell, Jim Tietz, David Winkler, Kristie Nelson, Melissa Pitkin, Missy Wipf, Claire Peaslee, Diana Humple, Ellie Cohen, David Wimpfheimer, Allen Fish, Nils and Sarah Warnock, David Lukas, Michael O'Brien, Louise Zemaitis, Ann Dewart, Heather Cameron, Keith Hansen, Jack Laws, and Stella Moss. There are many others: a deep bow to each of you.

My bird nerd friends, peers and mentors alike, who are a constant source of laughter and inspiration and the future of our field: Nora Livingston, Dan Maxwell, Zach Schlanger, Justin Hite, Chris McCreedy, Phil Chaon, Adam Searcy, Matt Brady, Ryan Terill, Andrew Guttenberg, Drew Lindow, and many others.

Thanks to the talented and dedicated team at Heyday: Gayle Wattawa, Molly Woodward, and Lindsie Bear for your patient, meticulous editorial work; to Diane Lee and Ashley Ingram for your patient, visionary design work; and to Christopher Miya for your email that fell out of the sky! And, of course, Malcolm Margolin, who I've never met, but whose fingerprints are everywhere.

I am indebted to Allen Fish and my other readers who lent their editorial and scientific advice to a young manuscript.

A shout out to the funky fresh ladies at The Foundry in Bozeman, MT, where I completed the second half of my manuscript: Kellie Sides, Tatum and Paige Johnson, Marley McKenna, and Eden Cooke.

Birds of Berkeley is a direct descendent of *A Field Guide to the Birds of Wesleyan:* the latter cannot exist without the former. Portraits of my team from Stethoscope Press at Wesleyan, Alec

Harris and Alex Ginsberg, hang above the mantelpiece of this work.

To my professors in the Art Studio Department at Wesleyan University—Julia Randall, Tula Telfair, Sasha Rudensky, and Laura Grey—who taught a science double major to see color, weight, and composition.

And, of course, to the millions of our fellow travelers and sojourners we call birds.

NOTES AND CITATIONS

GENERAL BIBLIOGRAPHY

Cornell Lab of Ornithology. Birds of North America. http://birdsna.org.

Cornell Lab of Ornithology. eBird. http://ebird.org.

Sibley, David Allen. *The Sibley Field Guide to Birds of Western North America*. New York: Alfred A. Knopf, 2003.

Richmond, Bob, Helen Green, David C. Rice, and Hans Peeters. *Alameda County Breeding Bird Atlas*. Berkeley, CA: Golden Gate Audubon Society and Ohlone Audubon Society, 2011.

AMERICAN ROBIN

Young, Jon. *What the Robin Knows: How Birds Reveal the Secrets of the Natural World*. New York: Mariner Books, 2013.

Solomon, Christopher. "When Birds Squawk, Other Species Seem to Listen." *The New York Times*. May 18, 2015.

On spectrographic equipment: A spectrogram (or sonogram) is a visual representation of the frequencies in a sound over time.

BLACK PHOEBE

Hindu *vahanas:* V., Jayaram. "Vahanas, the Vehicles of Hindu Gods and Goddesses." Hinduwebsite.com. http://www.hinduwebsite.com/vehicles.asp.

BUFFLEHEAD

Bay development and protection:

Poskanzer, Jef. "Berkeley Creeks." http://www.acme.com/jef/creeks.

"Don't Pave My Bay: History." Save the Bay. https://www.savesfbay.org/dont-pave-my-bay/history.

Schwartz, Susan. "History and Future of the Berkeley Waterfront" and "Restoring and Protecting Nature in the Eastshore State Park." Friends of Five Creeks. http://www.fivecreeks.org/history/Shorelinehandouts.pdf.

The West Berkeley Shellmound:

Dore, D. Christopher, Stephen Bryne, Michael McFaul, and Garry L. Running IV. "Why Here? Settlement, Geoarchaeology, and Paleoenvironment at the West Berkeley Site (CA-ALA-307)." *Proceedings of the Society for California Archaeology* 17 (2004): 27–33.

Berkeleyside reporting: http://www.berkeleyside.com/tag/west-berkeley-shellmound.

Indian People Organizing for Change: http://ipocshellmoundwalk.homestead.com/index.html.

BURROWING OWL

"Burrowing Owls." Golden Gate Audubon Society. Accessed April 2017. https://goldengateaudubon.org/conservation/burrowing-owls.

BUSHTIT

Sloane, Sarah A. "Bushtit." Cornell Laboratory of Ornithology. Birds of North America. January 1, 2001.

CALIFORNIA SCRUB JAY

Bakalar, Nicholas. "Welcoming the Newly Discovered." *The New York Times*. May 26, 2014.

Gonella, Paulo Minatel, Fernando Rivadavia, and Andreas Fleischmann. *"Drosera magnifica* (Droseraceae): the Largest New World Sundew, Discovered on Facebook." *Phytotaxa* 220, no. 3 (July 2015): 257–267.

Two distinct species: Kaufman, Kenn. "Here are the Biggest Changes to the AOU Checklist of North American Birds." National Audubon Society. News. http://www.audubon.org/news/here-are-biggest-changes-aou-checklist-north-american-birds.

CALIFORNIA TOWHEE

California Towhee Capital of the World: 797 California Towhees were detected within the Oakland CBC count circle in 2015, more than in any other. There were 784 found in 2016, hopefully enough to defend the title. For Oakland and San Francisco CBC reports, see: Golden Gate Audubon Society's website: https://goldengateaudubon.org/birding-resources/christmas-bird-counts. For countrywide data, see the National Audubon Society's database: http://www.audubon.org/conservation/science/christmas-bird-count.

CHESTNUT-BACKED CHICKADEE

Dixon, Keith L. "Some Ecological Relations of Chickadees and Titmice in Central California." *The Condor* 56, no. 3 (1954): 113–124.

Grinnell, Joseph. "A Second List of the Birds of the Berkeley Campus." *The Condor* 16, no. 1 (1914): 28–40.

Stallcup, Richard. "Chickadees on the Move...Slowly." *Point Blue Observer,* no. 41 (summer 1995): 6–7.

COOPER'S HAWK

Nesting: Pericoli, Ralph V. and Allen M. Fish. *GGRO's East Bay Cooper's Hawk Intensive Nesting Survey: 2003*. Golden Gate Raptor Observatory and Golden Gate National Parks Conservancy. May 2004.

Cooper's hawks and Sharp-shinned Hawks: Cooper's Hawks outnumber Sharp-shinned Hawks about ten to one during the nesting season, but only about two to one during winter and migrations. Allen M. Fish, email message to the author, April 10, 2017.

Most cost-effective pest-control technology: Raptors Are the Solution. http://www.raptorsarethesolution.org.

EUROPEAN STARLING

On Eugene Schieffelin releasing starlings: "American Acclimatization Society." *The New York Times*. November 15, 1877; and Gup, Ted. "100 Years of the Starling." *The New York Times*. September 1, 1990.

The Bard: Shakespeare, William. *Henry IV, Part I*. Act 1, scene 3, line 559: Hotspur seeks to antagonize King Henry by training a starling to repeat the name of Hotspur's brother-in-law Mortimer, whom King Henry refuses to ransom out of jail.

Kessel, Brina. "Distribution and Migration of the European Starling in North America." *The Condor* 55, no. 2 (1953): 49–67.

FORSTER'S TERN

Records in Alameda County: The most birds seen in one day in Alameda County was 172 on April 22, 2012, by Zachary Baer, Dominik Mosur, and Michael Park. The most birds seen in one year in Alameda County was 267 in 2008 by Bob Dunn. The most species seen in Alameda County in a lifetime was 396; Bob Richmond holds that record. For more information, see Joe Morlan's California County Birding Pages: https://www.fog.ccsf.edu/~jmorlan.

Blood mercury levels: Ackerman, J.T. "Mercury in Forster's Terns in Relation to Space Use of San Francisco Bay Habitats." USGS Western Ecological Research Center. March 2008. https://www.werc.usgs.gov/ProductDetails.aspx?ID=3565.

PBDEs in eggs: Cone, Marla. "Bay Seabird Has Record Level of Toxic Chemical." *Los Angeles Times*. September 10, 2004.

HERMIT THRUSH

"[T]he frozen stars...": Keats, John. "What the Thrush Said."

For another example of a thrush in English poetry, see: Hardy, Thomas. "The Darkling Thrush."

"Verdi or Mahler...": Oliver, Mary. "In Our Woods, Sometimes a Rare Music." *A Thousand Mornings.* New York: Penguin, 2013.

OAK TITMOUSE

Hetrick, Stacia A., and Kathryn E. Sieving. "Antipredator Calls of Tufted Titmice and Interspecific Transfer of Encoded Threat Information." *Behavioral Ecology* 23, no. 1 (2012): 83–92.

SNOWY EGRET

On the feather trade and the activists who ended it: Audubon. "History of Audubon and Science-Based Bird Conservation." http://www. audubon.org/content/history-audubon-and-waterbird-conservation. Also see Souder, William. "How Two Women Ended the Deadly Feather Trade." *Smithsonian Magazine.* March 2013.

WESTERN GULL

Pierotti, Raymond J., and Cynthia A. Annett. "Western Gull." Cornell Laboratory of Ornithology. Birds of North America. January 1, 1995.

Point Blue Conservation Science. Facebook post, July 3, 2014. https://www.facebook.com/PointBlueConservationScience/ posts/10152582068943674.

WESTERN MEADOWLARK

Whites only: Gammon, Robert. "Hidden Monuments to Racism." *East Bay Express.* September 20, 2017.

A sea of meadowlarks "three miles wide": Allen, Amelia. "Additional Notes on the Birds of a Berkeley Hillside." *The Condor* 45, no. 4 (1943): 149–157.

Grinnell, Joseph. "A Second List of the Birds of the Berkeley Campus." *The Condor* 16, no. 1 (1914): 28–40.

WESTERN SANDPIPER

Wilson, W. Herbert, Jr. "Western Sandpiper." Cornell Laboratory of Ornithology. Birds of North America. January 31, 2014.

Roberson, Don. "Monterey Birds: Nuttall's White-crowned Sparrow." http://creagrus.home.montereybay.com/MTYbirdsWCSP1.html.

Dialects vary mile by mile: Todd, Kim. The Language of Sparrows: How Bird Songs are Evolving to Compete with Urban Noise." *Bay Nature.* January 20, 2016.

The vanguard of a dwindling population: Sadly, the population once historically found in the Berkeley hills may be locally extirpated, probably due to habitat loss. Although this is most likely driven by human development, it is worth noting that fog has decreased in coastal areas of California over the last few decades, likely due to climate change, which may potentiate a number of cascading ecological changes. Is less fog reaching the upper canyons of the Berkeley hills? What does this spell for our local ecology? For Nuttall's? Around Berkeley, Nuttall's White-crowned Sparrows can be reliably found west of San Pablo Avenue, where there is thick, regular fog and healthy stands of Coyote Bush. See: Johnstone, James A., et al. "Climatic Context and Ecological Implications of Summer Fog Decline in the Coast Redwood Region." *Proceedings of the National Academy of Sciences of the United States of America* 107, no. 10 (2010): 4533–4538.

WRENTIT

Cornell Laboratory of Ornithology. "Wrentit." All About Birds. https://www.allaboutbirds.org/guide/Wrentit/id.

The world ultramarathon title: Newcastle University Press Office. "Record-breaking Bird Migration Revealed in New Research." June 7, 2016. http://www.ncl.ac.uk/press/news/2016/06/arcticterns.

ABOUT THE AUTHOR

Oliver James was born in Berkeley, California, in 1991. He started watching birds in his backyard on Colusa Avenue at age five and never turned back. Since then, he has competed in national birding tournaments, worked as a birding tour guide, and joined ornithological research teams from Peru to Alaska. He graduated from Berkeley High School in 2009 and Wesleyan University in 2014, and in 2021 he received master's degrees from the Energy and Resources Group and the Goldman School of Public Policy at UC Berkeley. James is also the author of *A Field Guide to the Birds of Wesleyan* (Wesleyan University Press, 2014). For more about his work, visit www.oliver-james.com.